AF483698

Root Reminders

JD Maresco

For Elliott and Jack, my greatest teachers.

Only two kinds of people can attain self-knowledge: those who are not encumbered at all with learning, that is to say, whose minds are not over-crowded with thoughts borrowed from others; and those who, after studying all the scriptures and sciences, have come to realise that they know nothing.

— Sri Ramakrishna

He called a little child to him, and placed the child among them. And he said: "Truly I tell you, unless you change and become like little children, you will never enter the kingdom of heaven."

— Jesus

Introduction.. 1

Childish Hope

Destiny 5

Cathedral 7

Bowing 9

Crisp 11

Bricks 13

Inherited 15

Jeans 17

Imaginal 19

Burn the Latch 21

Luminous 23

Mythic River 25

Dark Faith

Birth... 29

Between Two Worlds 31

Haunt 33

Wildness 35

Cliff 37

Relentless 39

The Fire 41

At Attention 43

Passing 45

Newborn 47

Scream 49

Breathless 51

Empty Love

Electric 55

Stillness 57

On Seneca Rocks 59

Glory 61

Conspire 63

NY Slice 65

Letting Go 67

Joy 69

Wisdom 71

A New Confession 73

I see poetry as a little energetic sketch of a moment in
time. Like all art, it finds its source material directly in the
wild and weird aspects of our daily lives. As a writer,
when I put pen to paper (or finger to screen), what
emerges generally feels like it could only have been
written in that precise moment. Words and time are
inescapably linked.

In writing a poem, I envision that I am first and foremost
producing medicine for myself. When I return to a poem
I wrote in the past, I re-enter that energy and learn to
accept a particular movement of my life. I think and hope
that, with time, this is helping me integrate the paradoxes
of existence.

Barry Taylor said that "God is the name of the blanket we
put over mystery to give it shape." Poetry is a little like
that to me, too. It never fully grasps truth, but tries to
place little markers around the edges of our experience as
we wind our way through the forest. Our journeys are
uniquely our own, but it seems we're ultimately in the
same forest. So I think it's reasonable to hope that our
poetry can be medicine for each other, too.

With a few exceptions, these poems emerged during a
roughly two-year period of intense grappling with my
identity and with reality itself. Many deal with deep
inquiry about the past and the passing down of trauma.
They are grounded in an attempt to re-examine these
aspects of the self — owning and disowning, reclaiming
and releasing. They embrace the idea that we can
appreciate reality and beauty only once we're willing to
accept it in all its forms. Perhaps most important to me,
they touch time and again on the counterintuitive wisdom

of children, and the appearance of truth in the most unexpected places.

The sections are organized — loosely — around themes, although there are common threads throughout. Many of the poems under *Childish Hope* embody movement towards my deepest darkness, as I've reckoned with the influence of growing up in a religious cult that introduced me both to life-changing encounters with spirit as well as gut-wrenching, destructive fear — of the world, of my body, and of my own intuition. *Dark Faith* puts words to the disorienting aftermath of facing up to that fear head on, and the underworld journey it seems we must go through on the path to real freedom. Lastly, in *Empty Love* I collected a series of poems that lean into the simplicity and joy of a surrendered life.

I am grateful you've taken the time to open this book. If one of these poems speaks to you, it'll be worth whatever time I spent putting it out there.

May you find peace and remember love.

— JD Maresco, February 2026

Childish Hope

I had a recurring dream as a child:
a purple blob of alien fear,
floating where the sermoner should stand spotlit,
    in the sanctuary, center stage.

That fear owned my visions,
morphing into feverish nights,
until I watched a holy man heave behind the curtain.

For years yet, I'd reflect on absence,
my inability to orbit the reasons
for good not to overcome evil all at once,
while they planted rhythmic mantras, dreamlike
into nascent minds, crowed open
by true encounter with spatial longings,
partially born again into an older melody,
but unwilling to hang full-throated
on the arm of grace.

Who — what — took away my stains, but
demanded the tenth part?

I watched you on the raised platform,
displaying the hands of passion
while I gave a quarter of my teenage earnings —
    and most of my heart —
    to help spread salvation.

I now know I hold the power
to evict my own sunk years,
bidding for the administration of medicine
from heroes with hearts unhealed.

And yet,

I've come to wonder:

Can the fruit that saved or slayed me in a past life
be the thing I must now devour?

If we have not come too late to the harvest,
maybe the story can still save us,
with all of its pertinent beauties,
    and hesitance,
    and proclamations of doom.

I eat the words,
I face the fear,
    letting your centuries of power drip down my bones,
and with the last drop of sacramental wine,
    I declare atop the ruins of our holy cathedral:

        I am the calling of Elisha
            as he summoned down the bear,
        I am the child on your knee,
            and the beggar's empty stare,
        I am the light of the weary world,
            and the birds of the open air,
        I am the universe on fire,
            the unraveling – and the permanence –
            of every prayer.

Beneath omnipotent spires, reformers stand
holding somnolent scrolls with staid dignity,
hovering gaze, prelates of stone,
knowing not where our future is prone,
with rhetoric cast in a hypnotic tone
known in the bones of centuries, yet
paying no mind to the red-vested cardinal
content to make its home in the branches.

No ordinary Episcopal, I am a boy, bored,
thumping the wooden boards of my pew
like some tribal horde, beating drums
made of skin stretched over hollow gourds,
bearing the brutal chorus
until my will is broken open with a blessing.

I am no longer young, but I still reason like a child,
the engine body torn down,
but the rolling stock kept greased and ready.
My feet flick and clack over the oak sleepers,
fastened firmly to levitate over the raised ballast,
the only freight on your express line,
still stopping here for your sanctuary,
and there for your punctuated reminders.

I have a sense to escape the mind formed in your court,
and another to find my bliss in its melancholic hollows,
but to reason with this mind now will do you no good!

Just bring me your latest translation of the mystic vision,
or your dissertation on the revival of lineage,
or your statistics on the rise and fall of the youth!

I won't disavow our myths,
or hold the law in derision —
I just know more glory in the gaze of a young girl
than the cups you swirl in your sacristy.

I'll drink what you hoist to my lips,
just grant me a voice like this beautiful bird,
while I hold a thread of your vestments,
like lacecaps holding last year's perennial petals,
to gently cover the beauty I am birthing beneath.

Limp strands of silver maple,
overlong limbs falling, gracing
childlike on waterlines, bowing
comatose with too much sun

as I did when I was eight:
hiding from Sunday school teachers,
    laughing,
    pretending to be enraptured by the divine

        and maybe I was

as I did in Flatiron:
hot summer air leaking in the window,
    groaning,
    bent over a toilet after so much fun

        and maybe it was

They should probably prune you
before the whole branch comes off

The swan doesn't really care either way

If winter cold could crisp like your words,
contracting vascular amplitudes,
frosting over my freedom,
sending messengers through my xylem,
from the tip of my snowy needles,
    to my hibernated root –

I still would not blame you — for
    retreating into safer woods, or
    parting from your fathers' foundation, or
    seeking strength in your sons' stature.

How hard you tried!

But we have shifted roots toward open spaces,
to air that lifts as we settle in solid stone,
reaching and shedding the vine,
the grasping matapalo,
strangling (without angst)

Ride along, if you will,
to the sunny hillside over the eastern sea,
    where suns set incessantly –
    placid breakers weaving waves of illumination,
    no goal in sight,
    no shore to reach

We are a swelling heartbeat,
in countless vantages

Can you see the horizon
from my branches?

How is it that bricks can
        stay
        stacked
        standing in formation

on a towering façade
for a hundred, say
    a thousand years

and my grandmother's mother
    could not rise from her bed?

if you cannot feel
if you do not notice your limbs
if the world does not move you like
your mind tells you it should

it may simply be

that someone who couldn't feel

told you that you shouldn't

in an age past

let your palms fly

   let them follow the reverend wind

      as it breaks your heart

all my jeans are ripping,
this one on the leg,
not the crotch like the others, already
well-worn to paper thin.

rip me like imitation silk,
from all corners, unraveled
thread recycled, raw, puréed
sinew by sinew,
form fresh to flawless tapestry

as I was

at some point, often in the forges of suffering
most of us have the opportunity to surrender vigorously
to who we actually are
deep in our imaginal core

this is a painful and lightful proposition
and I wonder if it is at the very core of the human journey

when I finally acknowledge that my intricacy
was held by someone who could not love me
    like I must love myself
molded out of duty or default
always towards an ideal

but I am not an ideal

and there is no other path

than to fall into my own visions

this is the scene where
we find out if he learns
that the whole plot is flipped on its head

the knot in your chest?
it hoards your treasure

they tried to teach us with words
but you can't learn her that way

burn the latch slowly with your loving gaze
like a cat, lying in wait, night after night
(as if you could steal what is already yours!)

each side
    of a luminous edge
from highest reach
    returning to bend

my keel won't even
begin to tell me

your eyes adopt my flesh,
your fire blazes from my fingers

we are writing our myths, you and I —
on the back half of this hill
that quickstops our valley of its youth

first sight, purple hyacinth
red, sandy soil
snakeless, thick, county turf
raising ingenerate voices life-unwise:

— don't go!

(a siren sounds)

— that hill is not meant for climbing!

(an in-breath)

— relax!

(I avoid an escalation)

— your time is not bent for seeking news!

(an out-breath)

you and I heard it, quiet and sacred,
not taught verbwise, but forged in family fire —
too alchemic to climb beside,
(although we stood handside for a loving time)

it was yours to know,
     and mine to find,
          and theirs to fear

where, combing through tunnels of stone, and
barehanded blasting,
remnants from rocky bankments torn,
I slaved and slivered on the mall

>> time discordant >>

birds alight on a trickling bank
flowers gird familiar temples
dawn softer than first grade summer
a child's carefree laugh

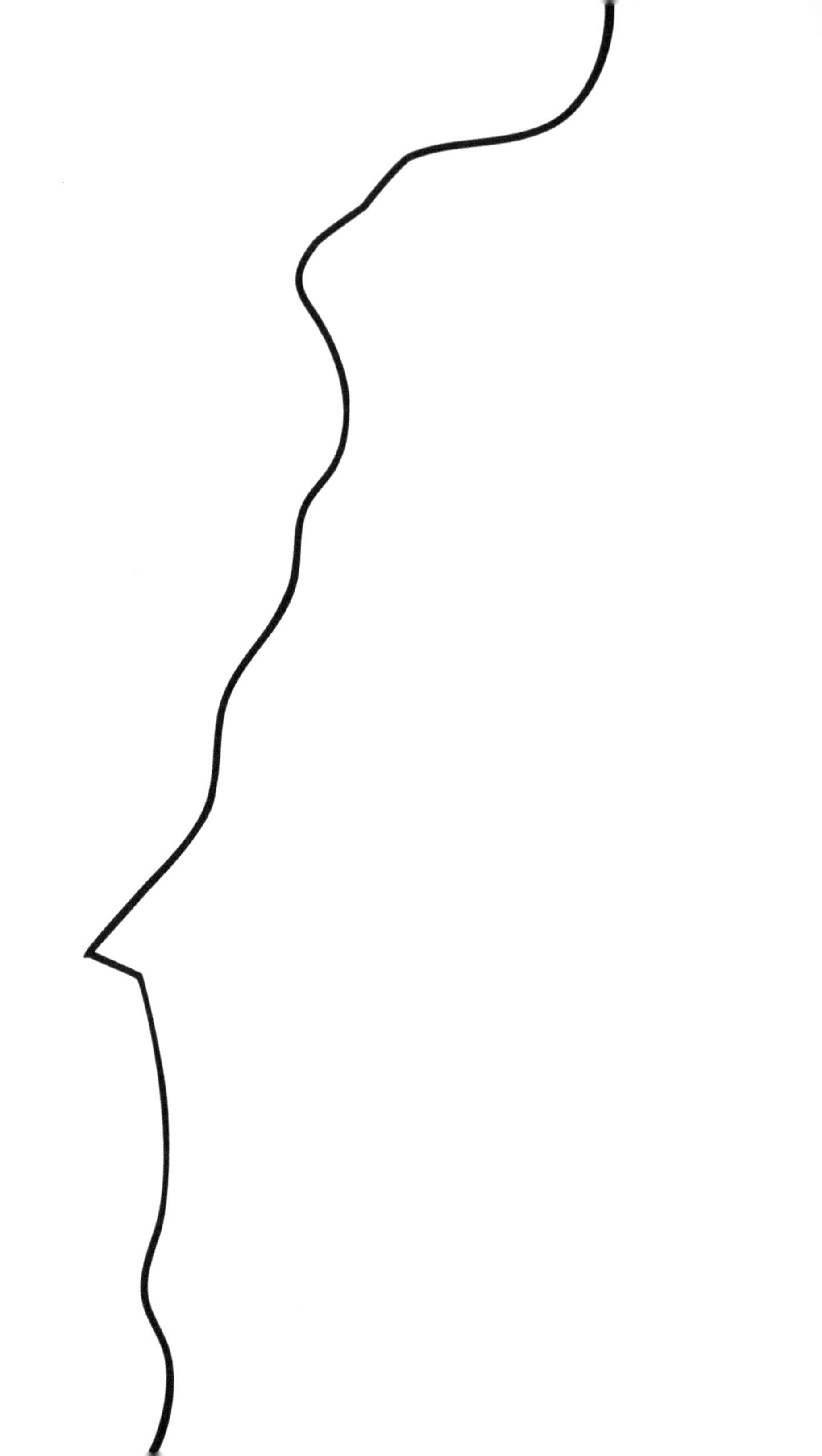

Dark Faith

righteously they rise!
from the terrible toil of mother,
and the broken hem of her garment

listless passion heard through the halls,
    flail of fingers,
    bursting breath,
    water and blood

when the moment arrives,
what else is there to do but give birth?

no goddamn injections or wires,
    we're doing this
    in the privacy
    of our present pain

welcome to this wild improvisation:

some little wordless path surrendering to things,
and the tender side of she who hides

oh take this cup from my claws!
I cannot bear it but I cannot let it go.
my other hand clenching
    the limb that casts
    its shadow over the eddy,
a slip from the torrent

I came for a pleasure ride,
you gave me a token and a time to arrive –
the lightning met me on the banks
as I leaned into your chest;
you lured me in with your playful gaze

where can I go from this being?
and when can I give him up?
is that you, mother, parading as the storm cloud,
ravishing the river so I lose my grip?

I long for your embrace,
but I cannot bear your forms!
you dance as endless light,
and I am caught in your terrifying vibration!

between two worlds

will you reverse this cup?
will you tear off my skin?
or will you cast me into the darkness?

will you shower me with your promise again?
or am I just a page in your book?
am I alone to bear your insatiable hunger?

I am a child,
shaking in your presence,
holding every precious stone and silly game
    you ever gave me.

oh mother! I wait in longing for you!

jai ma
jai jai ma

om gate gate paragate parasamgate bodhi svaha
om gate gate paragate parasamgate bodhi svaha

sometimes I think

the things that haunt us

won't let us be

until we let them be

and surrender to the storm

which turns out to both

be the thing we feared

and the thing we always longed for

we're more afraid of wildness
than any specter haunting the edges of our perception:
the child running circles in the clothing store,
a profane word uttered in the sanctuary –
god forbid!

my aunt said she saw a demon in her living room,
but I met its dark presence in my own body,
and before I awoke with the dawn,
my love reached out to kiss its feet as it fled.

there are more of them than you think –
these luminous progressions,
grandiose hands reaching, dancing –
we pass them on like syndromes,
and bleed them out again.

∞

in another place:
your foot grazes a stream,
the scent of amaranth rises on a subtle breeze,
fields of endless blossoms stretching to the east,
devouring the warming light.

you collapse into such earth as you are made of
and have no thought of demons nor angels,
because they have not yet emerged from your side.

on a cliff's edge,
the leading of the riverpath
probing valleys and peaks
with frantic eyes

what pulled me on?
where from here?

the voice whispers:
    everything that advances must also rewind
    the essence comes in the first act
    return to childlike wonder

is this a planted seed
or the root of me?

I think I know this way,
but am I willing to be rewound,
and at what cost?

I cannot decide
    if my assignment is to try on these new clothes,
    or to take them off for good

grieve grieve grieve!
what you have lived,
what you have loved,
and, most of all: your aching future

we are on a moving train
facing backwards,
glimpsing, for a moment, rotating forms
until they blur from view,
some alive,
some dead,
some asleep —
each pulled, death-on-birth

fiercely,
relentlessly,
effortlessly,

into the great waking beyond

when you start opening to the fire,

      the light
           pours
       in

the fire brings:

    mourning with power
    the tapping and closing of an ear
    saltwater sailing on the abyss
    entropy different than the one you know

chaos, loved

everything connects,
    I fear

it's a sip of coffee that tastes like yesterday

she said the same six words that I'm reading now,
torn out of a page and pasted in the laser sky.
"Ha! I get it, you want me to see you!"

I resonate for the moment like a frozen breath,
as still as rowed kernels shaking on the husk
which is to say: Not Very.

sun-beat, gorging, blasted by light from all sides,
she takes a mouthful and mumbles:

"I know someone's trying to get my attention,
but I don't know what my attention is."

what is this moment I have come to fear?
a fire I've known since waking on this path
the bloody prism owned without repair
the pain I chose within a blazing laugh

her movement through the flame of earthly state
you whisper in my ear the signs I need
to burn among the skulls of love and hate
the word that shakes and breaks me in the knees

throwing off my clothes in Varanasi
following the current to the buried
hold me while I turn to face my passing
I know with little doubt that I am carried

there's something falling on the fault line again
"still, aware" they describe the body
caught on the crevice before I crash the case

a finger untraceable,
    lifting untenable
        passion - unknowable

gone! — before the stars track me down

let's dust off the mind movements,
you peer over the yawning precipice
while I sweep the sandforms

.

.

.

there's no one here.
what the trembling hell?

the waves of my salvation are passing through,
up and out of a warming chest –
a shift, a mark, down an unknown meridian,
anchoring my aching back body,
I allow the newborn scream:

I am cradled desperation!
I am surrendered liberty!
I am inevitable magic!
I am magnetized blood!

I've learned there are things worse than heartbreak,
like knowing you have poetry inside you,
    lock-kneed, unable to kick in the dam
    to face the torrent of your life

then:
    a guttural scream, containing
    all ten thousand emotions you felt before dinner

the novels,
    the elegies,
    the prayers of the saints too are filled
with subtly-desperate, often-wordless pleas
shaking the feet of the unknown soul

to bare its teeth and tear into us
    with the brute clarity of a hundred hurricanes,
    leveling the foundation as we knew it –
    earth rent, pale, inconsequent

we take our tender, bruised backs
down to the soft, cedar soil
burrowing tired heads into pillowed moss
while a sea of stars breathe down on us

you saw the gem once, did you not?
her timeless light uncontained,
unequivocally free and blissful,
blossoming as one with your rapt awareness
at the base of your hollowed heart?

oh, she can leave you breathless —
as if a hand lurches to grab you by the chest,
like a mother reaching for a lost child,
there will be no life until she is again held tight

but even if you sell what you think you own,
you cannot buy that pearl,
only claim the field in which you lie,
the realm you already now inherit

hear this:
    unless you grasp what you already have,
    you cannot find what your mind reaches for

so may you jettison worlds,
    homes,
    loves,
    even your own name

may you rise with your own two feet
as you hold the power in that stillness

may you be carried on the brilliant rhythm
    of the dance that is you,

        and find, in her, worlds without end

Empty Love

does it ever feel so electric,
you can't possibly fathom the magic it would take
for eight billion others to share
the exquisite attention that she gives you?

holding, dancing, uplifting every blade of grass
as if, from the seed,
blown across some pointless field,
it landed at the very place you would dig today

growing in its senseless glory,
dancing in its causal surrender,
reaching to some all-encompassing sky

it lifts a single finger,
not caring if you look to where it points:

a billion galaxies spinning for me,
conspiring to worship at my feet (and yours),
while I kiss your face goodnight
and watch you drift home

there are countless things that we call love

beyond all of them
(I think, as I do)
I am chasing a wordless pull
forward, through, then back to bloodlines

past all definitions of
    companionship,
        self-sacrifice, and
            desire

to the melodic, turning stillness that claims my aim
without ever saying its name

an ineffable draw,
even and especially through the turning of
    bliss, terror, and boredom

bloom to breath to burn,
revelation to rest,
ten thousand times

light to dark
to light

to dark

to

the one who grabs alone the sky of god,
and finds the magic in the life mundane,
    and chooses serving oatmeal while it's hot,
    and grasps the majesty of summer rain,
    and light refracting through a dirty pane
knows more than any ashram ever taught

I find that joy is curious and rare
reasoning with subtle invitations
    sitting in your bed to brush your hair
    asking me to build a Lego station
    weary battles of negotiation
the mystery of life is in repair

the wearing of attention as a sword
the engine of our striving finding rest
    in quiet love's collision breaking forward
    this little burst is broker of the best:
    a token of a fragrant world possessed,
the bliss the evergreen is reaching toward

the poetry I want to be replies
not to the transcendental, but to flesh

An eminent scholar, I am first in class,
the rejuvenation of a generation!
We are latent revelation in the waiting,
making our collective parents proud.

Setting the world on fire,
rising through the retinue to some place of greater good,
    authority,
in store for the keepers of
    time, of
    morality, of
    everything they struck us to know.

Now a child is born,
and I face his graces and griefs in the same measure —
self-knowledge lacking or rising in the same cadence,
fading as I brace for a new dawning,
yawning through breakfast and bedtime.

Can I prevent a concurrent collapse?
Or shall I bridle my bit,
flinging myself into some self-same stream,
reliving the romance and the ritual of youth,
the relief and the call?

I choose to lose most
	of the confounding corporal handbook,
as I step in the rush of the river.

Like a Coho caught in the wrong season,
you revive me with a swift fish motion of the wrist,
gracing me to swim on
to the place of my birth,
the palace of my passing.

My boy, you are the harker of a new heaven!
You are the proclamation of the mundane.

I am not here to teach you facts,
I am only here to speak glory.

do you, too, feel the whole world conspiring to carry you?

surely our paths are woven together in mysterious ways

An upper-middle-aged, Middle Eastern man
    pulling a shawarma cart

A young Black woman
    smiling at a niche comedy podcast

Tourists with selfie sticks
    posing in front of a pizza shop

A nanny with a stroller
    turning the corner precisely on time

A government worker with a stretch lanyard badge
    stress-walking out of the courthouse

A taxi driver, leaning on his car
    staring at the skyscraper sunset, smoking

20-somethings who are barely making rent
    kissing at the stairs to the Hoyt Street station

My desire for this earth threads the erotic

I want to be inside these faces

Let's lie here and talk about our intersections,
     moan our suffering into sunsets,
       bring the world into the motion of our bodies,
     as we dance our love into the void

Am I more than my atoms?

The way I feel for this chaotic world
makes me want to scream yes

sex is a radical act of letting go

coincidentally, so is love

allowing:
conflagration of bones, threaded
loosely through the other, yet to dance away
with fingers clawing, flesh sifting
through the outer layers of the atmosphere
until Jupiter breaks free of all its salient reasons
    for being in orbit

tethering:
to the product of some primordial fling
between the sun and its centripetal muses
eyes deep as the reaches of a neighboring galaxy
an invisible nebula churning
I, a still, pulsing atom,
dancing inevitably with the universe

you take joy

in a thousand tiny candles

they will burn out in a day

as ten thousand more

alight in your bones

the fear of being is the beginning of wisdom

love of being is its end

love of being is its end

all-embracing nature,
I confess I am drawn irresistibly to your beauty

my mind is wandering again
my thoughts are drawn to today's transactions
my words are often half-truths
my deeds get stuck in the patterns of the past

I am learning to love it all
as I learn to love myself
I rest in silence
and gently acknowledge the perfection of what is

I release my grip
as I turn back towards lovingkindness
for the sake of the light that is dawning in me

may we have mercy on our fragile bodies
and stand up to heal each others' wounds

that we may delight in the way things are
and be vessels for your flow
to the glory of being

amen